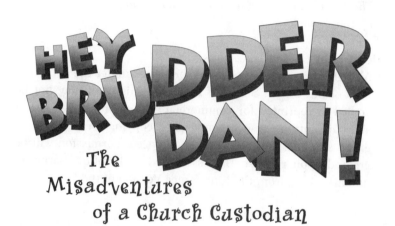

HEY BRUDDER DAN!

The Misadventures of a Church Custodian

DAN ZYDIAK

Hey, Brudder Dan!
The Misadventures of a Church Custodian
by Dan Zydiak

ISBN 1-58169-020-7
For Worldwide Distribution
Printed in the U.S.A.

Evergreen Press
An Imprint of Genesis Communications, Inc.
P.O. Box 91011 • Mobile, AL 36691
(800) 367-8203
Email: GenesisCom@aol.com

TABLE OF CONTENTS

INTRODUCTION

The stories you are about to read are true except for the eighty percent I made up. The names of those mentioned have been changed to protect me legally and to keep them from coming over to my house...to pay me a "friendly" visit. I hope you enjoy this book a lot. If you do, please go back to your bookstore and buy two more copies to give to your friends. If you don't have any friends, this is an excellent way to make some.

If you don't find my book funny, put it down, because you are probably in a bad mood. In a few days, you will feel better and it will seem hilarious to you. If that doesn't work, see your doctor immediately—something is dreadfully wrong with your funny bone.

When I took the job as church custodian, I intended it to be a temporary arrangement, but I had such a good time I hated to leave. (Remember what David said in Psalm 23: "And I shall dwell in the house of the Lord forever.")

My tenure at Springhill Avenue Baptist Church was an experience I'll never forget. My title said "Custodian" but my job description included whatever service was needed at the time.

Lots of times, I would see the humor in what was happening around me, or to me, and just laugh out loud. I hope this book will help you laugh a little, too.

DEDICATION

To Percy and Janie Sanderford
who live their beliefs—
thank you for your encouragement.

1

YELLOW DOG

Rain! I thought, as I looked up at the dark clouds gathering in the south. The humidity was high and the air oppressive. It was only June, but at 9:30 a.m. the temperature was already in the 90s. The Baptist church where I work, named after the street it faces—Springhill Avenue—was bathed in a haze of heat.

Springhill Avenue Baptist Church is a large church. Its gothic white columns towering high above the street are reminiscent of a great Southern past. The church has served Mobile, Alabama, in a proud, friendly tradition for 76 years.

I, too, am large, with brown hair, hazel eyes, and a

shape like a barrel. My name is Dan. Some of my duties include buffing the floor, dusting and waxing the furniture, taking out trash, and anything else anyone of the 400 members of the church can think up, such as turning a Sunday School Department for senior citizens into a banquet hall, or playing Santa Claus for the primary children. Some of my most challenging tasks are taking care of a tired old furnace and making sure an antiquated air conditioning unit doesn't stop running. However, when the latter fails to function, it tends to lend a dramatic effect to an emotional "fire and brimstone" sermon.

Handling "Yellow Dog," our infamous church bus, however, was a job in a class by itself. The first time I saw it, I wondered if I could handle it. It looked innocent enough—tires straight, yellow paint intact, though slightly dirty. Overcoming my apprehension, I threw open the squawking door, mounted the three metal steps, and slid into the driver's seat. At first glance, the controls looked as complicated as those you would find in the cockpit of an airplane. I had driven a dump truck in the Army and was somewhat experienced in the handling of large vehicles. But this vehicle was of a breed all its own.

As the readily available custodian of our church, I was the naturally expected volunteer to drive the bus. My first assignment was to pick up the "Jolly Elders" at the Crichton Towers, located about six blocks away, for their monthly meeting and "covered dish" lunch. I turned the key, and the engine started with a guttural roar. As I passed the bank, I noticed it was 9:46. As the meeting didn't start until 10:00, one minute wouldn't make much difference. I pulled the bus smoothly to the curb in front of the apartments and got out to assist my waddling, frowning group of female passengers on board. The first lady wore a large artificial corsage and greeted me with, "Late again!" This being my first time to drive, I simply smiled and ignored the remark. The second lady had a huge cameo pinned on crooked at the neck of her blouse. She stopped at the foot of the steps and looked me up and down. Noticing my somewhat oversized form, she asked, "Will you be eating with us?"

"No, ma'am. I brought my lunch."

My third passenger wore a small, blue flowered hat. As she prepared to board, she thrust a clattering casserole dish into my hands. "Hold this," she said, using both hands to pull herself into the bus.

The last lady finally got on.

I took my place behind the wheel of the idling machine, put it in gear, and started with a little jerk. I looked into the overhead mirror and came to an immediate halt. One of the old darlings, who had paused to visit before sitting down, stood gripping the back of a seat, hat slung forward, knees bowed in a surfer's stance. An angry expression on her face met my gaze. I waited until she was seated before attempting another start.

It soon became quite evident how Yellow Dog got its name. In the crowded traffic, the bus began the shake and rattle. When it backfired, the wheels felt as if they had left the ground. At this, the mumbling in the back became louder. I heard someone say, "It never sounded like this when Pete drove." Old Pete, the former custodian, had quit while he was ahead. As the traffic became more congested, Yellow Dog, with its tailpipe between its back wheels, died on Springhill Avenue, hugging the curb as if it were afraid to venture out into the snarling traffic.

"What's the matter with the bus?"

"It's probably nothing. The bus is just old and needs a little coaxing."

"First he's late, and now this," said a little blue-haired lady with arms folded and foot tapping.

Turning to offer further apology, I found, only inches from my face, two pink cheeks and wide blue eyes filled with concern. Speaking loudly, the lady with the cameo brooch asked, "Should we start walking? How long will we be stuck here?"

"As long as it takes," I mumbled to myself.

"What?"

"I'm sure if you will just be a little patient, we'll be on our way soon."

"Well, my chicken is getting cold."

I pumped the gas and turned the key. The bus belched black smoke and rumbled back to life. Turning the corner beside the church, I overshot my mark by about eight feet, because the rear wheels were still in the middle of the street. As I started to back up, I looked in the mirror only to find the same lady (with the blue flowered hat) gripping the back of the seat, hat over one eye, legs bowed, as she asked, "Will YOU be driving us back?"

That afternoon, on the trip back to the Towers, I noticed there was no dawdling in the aisles. Everyone was seated as I got on the bus. During the meeting, it had rained, and before we had reached our destination, the bus had splashed through numerous puddles. Coming to our first red light, I applied the brakes, which grab when they

4

are wet, and threw everyone forward. I dared not look back for fear of retribution. The absolute silence and chill in the air told me that I had really fallen from grace this time. Upon our arrival, I stopped in front of the apartments and waited expectantly for their departure. No one moved. Having learned not to stand up too quickly on my bus, they were being cautious. The lady with the flowered hat was the last to leave.

Two weeks later, there was a pastor's conference at our church. Among the men attending was a short, brown-skinned Brazilian by the name of Manuel. His clear Latin eyes were full of life and happiness. He was talking with Brother Johnson, my pastor, as I walked up with a question about the air conditioner.

"What we would like eez to have your bus and for you to provide us weeth a driver." Brother Manuel spoke slowly, pronouncing his words carefully. He was in charge of the International Mission, and every Friday night, its doors open to the foreign children of Mobile. Churches that participate in this service volunteer one night a month to pick up children and drive them to the mission. The good Reverend Johnson looked at me and smiled. Turning back to Manuel, he said, "I think I have just the person you're looking for."

"Of course . . . I'll be glad to do it," I replied.

"Thank you, Brudder Dan. We be looking for you every third Friday night." After we shook hands to seal the agreement, he left in search of a fourth person.

On Monday of the third week, I received a call from Manuel. "Brudder Dan?"

"Yes, speaking."

"Theese eze Brudder Manuel. I'm calling to remind you of theez Friday night."

"Yes, I remembered, and I'm looking forward to it. By the way, how will I know which apartments in the complex to stop at?"

"Don't worry. The children . . . they weel be coming when they seez the bus."

"Will there be someone from the mission to go with me?"

"The Lord . . . He go weeth you."

"Right."

The fateful Friday night came all too quickly, and I found myself sitting once again behind the wheel of Yellow Dog. Now when the bus hadn't been used in a while, it was sometimes hard to start. Before I turned the key, I said a quick prayer, "Lord, let it start the first time."

I turned the key, and nothing happened. I tried once more and still nothing. I uttered another quick prayer while looking down at the dirty floor. "Lord, just let the battery get an easy jump from my car."

Getting down, I got my jumper cables from the trunk of my brown Ford, which was parked conveniently next to the bus, and proceeded to attach the cables to the bus and my car. I started my car, and then tried starting the bus. Nothing happened. Moths circled the streetlight above the bus. A dog barked in the distance. Again I prayed. "Lord, send help."

At that moment, a stranger walking down the street wearing a tee shirt and blue jeans stopped to help. He seemed to have some knowledge of mechanical things. After doing something to the cables, he said, "Try it now." I did, and it started immediately. I thanked him as I put away the cables, and was soon on my way. "Thank you, Lord."

On the way over, I pulled up to a light next to some teenagers in a black '57 Chevy. The passenger, a blonde-haired boy of perhaps 18, yelled up at me, "Wanna drag?" He revved up the motor as he and his friend laughed. Something devilish came over me, and with my left foot still on the clutch, my right foot pumped the accelerator a couple of times. Yellow Dog screamed and the noise drowned out the black machine completely. I looked down and smiled wickedly as their laughter ceased. The light changed and the car squealed off, leaving me and the dog behind. Well, we had beat them in noise anyway.

Turning into the apartment complex was like entering a foreign country, me being the only native-born American in sight. The Cambodians stood or squatted in front of their apartments. All of the windows and doors were open, everyone trying to catch a cool evening breeze. The culture was clearly evident in their dress and environment. The men wore khaki shorts and no shirts or shoes. Two of them were standing on the sidewalk talking. As they heard the bus approach, they turned and watched with suspicion when I entered their domain. I smiled and nodded. They returned my greeting with a slight bow, relieving my apprehension somewhat. Some of the people had planted small gardens in their front yards and had put up cardboard fences, made from large boxes, to protect them from the children and dogs. I approached the last section of the complex, and children came running from all directions, clamoring to get on the bus. Opening the bus door, I noticed there had been a fire in one of the buildings. By this time, a torrent of children were pouring into the bus. Some, less than a year old, were in the care of an older brother or sister. The oldest were in their early teens. They numbered about 42. All were talking or screaming—some in broken English, others in a language unknown to me.

"Hey, man. We go now. Okay?"

"Okay," I replied.

I smiled and turned to my left to put on the lights as darkness was coming soon, only to come face to face with a youngster of about five. He had climbed over the rail and sat perched on the box by the controls, smiling at me with enormous brown eyes. He was wearing a red baseball cap sideways on his head and a sweatshirt that read, "New York Yankees." I asked my little friend what had happened to the building that was burned. His answer was not what I expected.

"This guy . . . he brought his girlfriend home and played his stereo too loud."

We reached the intersection at Azalea Road and found four lanes of cars racing past us. I spotted a break in the traffic, popped the clutch, and floored it. We moved out, swaying more than a little. From the back of the bus, I heard, "just like the Duke boys." The small boy sitting beside me had turned on the heater switch, which added to the already sweaty condition of the overcrowded bus. I turned off the heater and said "No" to my little co-pilot, but I was barely audible above the roar of the other passengers.

We had neared the corner of Dauphin and McGregor. I turned the wheel, and the bus swayed onto Dauphin, heading down a long hill. The added weight of 42 children was not taken into account when I had chosen this route. The bus began to increase in speed rapidly, with little effort on my part. A blue Volkswagen pulled lazily into our lane, about 30 yards ahead of Yellow Dog, apparently admiring the scenery and completely unaware of the larger vehicle approaching. I automatically hit the brakes, to no avail. Sweat clouded my vision on the left. The children were becoming more excited at the prospect of squashing the bug before us. I wiped the water from my face and glanced into the left rear-view mirror to check for clearance. A white Toyota was approaching fast. With no time to be polite, I took my foot off of the non-effective brake and eagerly applied the gas pedal. I swerved, barely missing the beetle and infuriating the Toyota. The action brought on a loud blast from the horn of the white car and cheers from the children as we passed the surprised Volkswagen. I felt only relief.

Within 20 minutes, we were turning onto Texas Street, where the mission is located. It's about three blocks from the interstate and stands in an open field. To our left was a large metal building with church buses parked on one side. We had arrived. I pulled up before the glass doors, through which all of my passengers scrambled as fast as they could, leaving a blessed silence in their wake. I parked the bus and walked back to the building, whistling the theme song from "The High and the Mighty."

When I entered the mission, I was greeted with a sympathetic smile from a young blonde woman with a bad complexion, who worked there. I was to find out later that the group I had brought was the worst group they had—a minor point that Brother Manuel had failed to reveal to me. I found Manuel behind a counter, much like the ones you see in an airport.

"Hey, Brudder Dan, you brought the children. Good!"

"Yes, no trouble at all," I lied.

"The noise . . . did eet bother you?"

"No, I usually wear a hearing aid, but I left it at home." Manuel seemed to find this quite funny and headed toward his office, laughing. Somehow, I failed to see the humor involved.

About two-thirds of the bottom floor of the mission building is a gym with pool tables to one side. I might add that it is not required to use any particular end of the cue stick when playing here. There were about 100 children in the gym. Basketballs whizzed around and would sometimes land on a pool table, which would result in angry foreign words. I retreated to a more organized area of the mission: the TV room. There were 15 to 20 children sitting around watching the "Duke boys" trying to jump a river with the police in hot pursuit. Noise is not permitted in this room, and this rule is strictly enforced by the children themselves as they watch their heroes.

At 8:00 p.m., the children were called upstairs to the chapel, which was built to hold about 80 men and now held over 100 children and adults. They sang songs about God's goodness, heard a short message, and saw a film. By this time, it was 9:00—time to go home. My group and I left the same way we had come: screaming.

The mission had other functions which I was to learn about. About two weeks later, I was home watching TV on a Tuesday night. At 9:00 p.m., my wife called me to the phone.

"Hey, Brudder Dan, theese eze Manuel."

"Yes."

"We have some seamen here, and our bus eze broken down. They have to be back on their ships by 10:00. Could you come and bring your bus, pleeze?"

"Well, I suppose I could. Yes. All right, I'll come."

A heartfelt "Graçias" followed. After I hung up, I stood by the phone wondering how I get involved in these situations. *Why couldn't I say no? After all, this really didn't concern me.*

I explained the call to my wife and headed toward the church. Yellow Dog stood ready, and for once, started on the first try. I made good time, arriving at the mission at 9:40. I left home in a hurry and hadn't taken time to change my clothes. I was wearing a blue baseball cap, a plaid shirt that was hanging out of a pair of bermuda shorts, and tennis shoes with no socks. Needless to say, I became an instant attraction when I walked through the door.

"Are you the cab driver?" a well-dressed lady inquired.

"No, I'm the bus driver. Where are the seamen?"

"They haven't come down from the chapel yet," said the woman from behind the counter. I was a little put out, having rushed and now being forced to wait. Since it was a hot night, I went out to the bus and let down the windows. The lobby was clearly visible through the glass doors. From the driver's seat, where I waited, I could see the seamen coming down. In a matter of seconds, the place was wall-to-wall with burly giants from many different lands. My preconceived notion of skinny sailors in white was quickly shattered. These people were three feet wide in the shoulders and well over six feet tall. They all looked like linebackers for a professional football team. . . . A mean team.

They began to lumber toward the bus. I started to whistle and thought to myself, "I'm going to die." They looked more than a little hard. About half of the men had scars on their faces, and the other half looked as if they had put them there. I smiled a lot and could feel myself start to sweat. Entering the bus, their cold stares sent chills up my spine. The bus was full, with three sailors standing in the aisle. A short, bald man from the mission had come along to give directions. His English, however, was limited to "left," "right," and "continue"—"continue" meaning to go forward.

We wound our way through the docks and then, going over the railroad tracks, Yellow Dog became bogged down. As I was gunning the motor, trying to get Yellow Dog to respond, a bright light appeared to my left. A loud whistle cut through the night. I thought to myself: "This can't be happening to me." Finally, with a spurt of energy, the bus rolled off the tracks just before the freight train rushed past. I turned to my guide, who was wiping his forehead and blowing out his breath at the same time—the international sign for narrow escape.

When all of the seamen were at their various ships, we drove back to the mission, where I found out that 12 of the men had found the Lord that night. Somehow, this information seemed to make it all worthwhile.

2
VISITATION

One of the most important activities of the Baptist Church is the visitation program. Not only does it reach out to the community for increasing the membership, it also lets those visited know that they are wanted and cared about. I participate in this daunting practice.

On Monday nights, a few battle-hardened prayer warriors would gather at the church and pair off. Each pair would select potential folks to visit whose names and addresses were written on 3"x5" cards. The teams of two each had some unwritten rules such as: the men teams would visit men, and the women teams would visit women, if possible. However, a mixed team could visit either sex without worry of offending anybody, unless the mixed team wasn't married. Then they would have a time limit based on the number of visits they planned to make, or take along a chaperone. Of course, if the mixed team consisted of, say, the youth director and a youth of the opposite sex, that would be okay; or the same with the pastor, choir director, assistant pastor, and church secretary.

There was one I remember in particular, an "Owen Potters" on Michigan Avenue—no phone. John and I were to be partners. John is a staunch Alabama fan—the man wears red socks with Bear Bryant's picture on them. He is a retired railroad man and full of life.

Michigan Avenue was once a very prestigious address close to the downtown section of Mobile. Around the turn of the century, those beautiful homes were nothing short of magnificent. But time and neglect had taken their toll. All of the descendants of those socially elite families have long since moved to the western suburbs. The Michigan Avenue homes remain standing, paint peeling and shutters askew, having been taken over in the most part by slum lords. These mercenary people have divided them up into small apartments and just do enough repairs to prevent one from descending through the bathroom floor in a clawfoot bathtub to the apartment below.

"Michigan Avenue. Hmmm. Pretty rough neighborhood," John said, reflecting as he held the orange 3"x5" card with Owen's name and address on it.

The pastor heard the apprehension in John's voice and said, "I know you and Dan can handle it."

"Oh, sure we can handle it. I could drop by my house on the way and pick up my .38."

"I have a .45," I said, wanting to let them know that I had a gun, too. John looked up and rolled his eyes. The pastor looked through his 3"x5" cards as if he had lost something. I felt proud that I had gotten to mention my gun.

So, John and I set out to find Mr. Potters, but without our guns. As we turned off Government onto Michigan, there was an air of excitement and danger. We had a feeling of being watched as John's car rolled slowly down the trash-strewn street lined with junk cars in the front yards. I noticed a man sitting in one, as if reminiscing about when his car had run, or at least had wheels. A dog was barking, and somewhere a child was crying. We stopped in front of the house. It seemed to lean somewhat to the left, but that effect was probably created by the shadows that caught the gables and balconies. Down the driveway, we saw a man in a lighted garage. Upon seeing our approach, the man quickly covered whatever he had been working on and hastily advanced to meet us. He was an older man with a large build and a rough face, made rougher by the fact that he needed a shave. His hair was grizzly, and looked white under the low glow of a nearby streetlight.

John was older than I, and we had come in his car, so I let him do the talking. "Do you know where we can find Owen Potters?"

"What's he done?"

"Nothing . . . as far as I know."

"Has he been complaining or something?"

"No."

"Are you two . . . cops?"

"No."

"I heard cops have to own up to it if they're asked."

"We're not from the Police."

"That's good, 'cause I don't want no trouble from the cops."

"We're from Springhill Avenue Baptist Church, here to see Mr. Potters."

"Well, don't preach at me. I sure am glad y'all ain't cops, though." With that, he turned his head toward an upstairs window where you could see the flickering light of a television set through the thin curtain and yelled, "Potters!" When there was no immediate response, he yelled again. "Yo, Potters!"

A moment later, a bald-headed man in his late 40s appeared at the window, and with some difficulty, managed to open it. The white-haired man yelled once more.

"Visitors for ya! They say they're not cops."

"What do you want?" the man yelled down to us in a shaky voice.

"We're from Springhill Avenue Baptist Church!" John yelled back.

"Okay, come on up!" the man yelled down to us, and closed the window.

As we turned to go inside, we heard the white-haired man mutter to himself. "Cops and preachers: Don't have no use for either one."

Upon entering the building, I noticed a musty odor of mildew, mixed with the scent of a wet dog. The dimly lit entrance revealed a trash-strewn hallway and a set of rickety stairs, with a small landing and a stout door at the top.

"That has to be Potters' place up there," I said, thinking aloud.

"Do you think so?" John asked slightly sarcastically. I didn't respond because I know John had been irritated by

16

the man outside. So, we went up the creaking stairs, with pealing wallpaper on the left, and a rickety railing on the right. John knocked on the door while I waited behind him on the stairs, as there was only room for one on the landing.

Owen opened the door and peered out at us. He paused long enough to decide we meant him no harm, then let us in.

As we came in, I noticed the walls were painted blue. The furniture consisted of an old brown over-stuffed chair with tears exposing some of the yellowed cotton stuffing, and a small black and white portable TV on a black metal stand. The other two doors besides the one to the stairs had to be for the bathroom and the bedroom. Those doors had once been painted white, but now looked dingy with dirty handprints, greasy smudges, and even red crayon marks—obviously from a former tenant.

All of a sudden, something hit the old wooden floor that seemed to slant. It rolled to a stop at my feet and looked like a top to a small spray can. As quick as he could, Owen gathered up the top and tried to reassemble and conceal his mace-like weapon with shaky hands.

"One can't be too careful," John said reassuringly. He went on to tell Owen who we were and what church we were from. Then he invited him to worship with us on Sunday.

Owen nervously explained that he was from a small town in north Alabama, where, if they have two shopliftings reported in the same week, the newspaper would run a story about their city having a crime wave. When he secured a job as head groundsman at a local school in Mobile, he was afraid of coming to the "big city," with its evil element and all. To heighten his apprehension, he had unwittingly moved into one of the worst sections of our town. Someone at work, who had resented his appointment, had also threatened him with bodily harm. Thus, this naturally timid man was so scared that the only time he would leave his shabby little apartment was either to go to work or to get something to eat. Now Burger King was the only restaurant near Owen's place, so that's where he got all of his food. But he wouldn't eat there, for fear of being spotted by one of his new enemies or of becoming a victim of a robbery. So he would carry it back to his little cubbyhole, like a mouse.

Upon hearing Owen's story and seeing his environment, I asked him if he would like me to drive over on Wednesday afternoon and take him to my home for dinner; then we could go to the Wednesday night prayer meeting. John didn't say anything, but I could see him thinking, at first, that I had lost my mind, then changing to approval, or even being proud of me. Owen was glad for a reprieve from his lonely lifestyle and decided to jump at the chance.

Normally, I would never invite anyone home without first consulting with my precious wife, because precious may become a little cranky, and I might find myself sleeping on the sofa. (Just kidding. She would never do that . . . Or would she?) When I explained to Gayle about Owen's plight and my invitation, she wholeheartedly agreed with my actions.

So, on Wednesday, after a delicious home-cooked Southern supper, we went to church, where Owen was greeted with the warmth and love that Baptist churches are famous for. He made many new friends that night, and became an active, faithful member of our church. In time, his wife joined him, and they took up housekeeping in a better neighborhood.

Owen and his wife never forgot the kindness that I had shown him in his first difficult days in Mobile. In our minds, it wasn't such a big thing that my wife and I had done for Owen; but it was to him, because that simple act of kindness had changed his world from being one of isolation in a strange town to being part of a loving fellowship, not to mention having been allowed to sample my wife's cooking.

3

CHURCH SOCIALS

Every Wednesday night, Baptist churches have a prayer meeting. We make these special occasions a part of our lives because we have so much joy when we're in the fellowship of other Christians that we find it hard to wait all the way until Sunday to experience it. On the third Wednesday of the month, we usually have a covered dish supper. However, it didn't take our pastor long to realize that when food was present, attendance improved. Therefore, he brought forth a motion to have a supper every Wednesday night; it was immediately seconded and voted in. The dinners would be provided at a modest price to cover the cost of the food. There would be no labor cost, as the meals would be cooked by rotating shifts of the ladies in the church. The ladies considered this a high honor.

Being the custodian, it was my responsibility to transform the senior adult department into a dining hall on Wednesday and back again before Sunday. I wasn't really unhappy about the task of lugging 10 heavy tables into a suitable arrangement, dragging the 80 chairs around, rolling out and cutting the table paper, and hauling in two clean garbage cans lined with black plastic bags. I just wasn't thrilled about the many times pastors or committee folks make decisions of grandeur and are congratulated on the fine job they had done when the venture comes to a successful conclusion, but fail to consider how their plans affected the custodian's already full schedule.

It was a hot day in June, and my son Billy and I were setting up the fellowship hall for the now regular Wednesday night supper. On occasion, my son would find the time to help me during the summer, especially if his mother told him to. As we were working on the tables, in walked Alice wearing a white uniform with the bottoms of her pants stuffed into heavy rubber work boots. Her hair was covered in a knitted cap she had pulled down over her ears. Her overall appearance was that of someone who worked in a meat locker. In all the years I have known her, she had always dressed in the same fashion. Her age was hard to determine. She stood about five foot seven, and had a ruddy, almost masculine, face. Her chunky, sturdy frame showed that she was no stranger to hard work. Because she had been deprived of adequate heat in her youth, she always dressed warmly; and in winter, she wore two heavy topcoats over her uniform and still shivered on moderately cold days.

"Come on, Billy, only two more tables and then we can start in on the chairs."

"Good morning, Dan . . . Good morning, Billy."

"Good morning, Alice," I replied, while Billy nodded politely in her direction.

"You guys setting up for a dinner or something?" The only thing that Alice liked better than warmth was food (she had probably been deprived of food as a child, too).

"Yes. From now on, there will be a dinner every Wednesday night."

"Well, that's good news. . . . You say every Wednesday night?"

"Yes . . . Is there something I can help you with?"

Alice's job was caring for Mrs. Allen, a 90-year-old invalid and one of the last surviving, founding members of the church. Back in the 50s, she had sold her property to the church for its expansion with the provision that the church move her house across the street on a small lot, where she could live the rest of her life rent-free.

"Oh, yeah . . . Mrs. Allen done fell out of her rolling chair, and I can't get her up."

The rolling chair was exactly that. It was like a wheel-chair, except that the back wheels were the same size as the small front ones.

Billy and I looked at each other for a half a second and both ran out the Hilen Avenue side door and across the street, with Alice laboring along behind. We found Mrs. Allen lying on the ground outside her house, holding her

22

dressing gown down for modesty's sake. The rolling chair lay beside her. As we stood there trying to figure out the best way to get her up, Alice came up and said, "There she is," proud of the fact that she had identified the lady for us. Billy and I exchanged smiles but said nothing except to inquire if Mrs. Allen was hurt. When we discovered she was unharmed, we eased her up (which was like trying to pick up a large slinky or an 80-pound water balloon) and carefully rolled her into the house. Alice thanked us as she took over her charge once more and rolled Mrs. Allen into a corner of the kitchen, facing the wall. Mrs. Allen didn't seem to mind; apparently she was just glad to be off the ground and out of the yard.

Billy and I returned to the church and resumed our work. It didn't take us long to complete the dinner arrangements.

I had to buff out the L-shaped hall that runs from the back door by the kitchen to the foyer off of the Hilen Avenue door, so I let Billy find amusement of his own while I worked on the hall. I loved to buff that old tile hallway because it was really beautiful when it was all shined up.

While I worked, my thoughts would wander back to a summer long ago, when I was between jobs and had gone down to the church to help Mr. Harvey. He had spent two days teaching me how to use the buffer. Mr. Harvey was an old saint who was happy in his work because he was helping to beautify the house of the Lord. He was known to sing praises to God as he worked—off-key, but definitely a joyful noise. He told me never to do anything the women wanted right away, because "They'll have you running every time they snap their fingers." I was advised just to finish what I was doing, or to wait awhile if I wasn't doing anything. With good reason, he warned me, "Never let them know you aren't busy, because, sure as the world, they will find something for you to do. Ain't nothing 'twill set a woman off quicker than to discover a man ain't got nothing to do," he would say.

I tried to beautify the house of the Lord just like Mr. Harvey did and was thinking about him when the back door slammed open. In the sudden glare from the floor, I couldn't see who it was until I heard the commanding voice of Mrs. Craig, the church secretary, yelling, "Billy, come get these cans off my car—I don't have time for this!"

At that moment, Billy came into the hall and said matter-of-factly, "It worked."

After Billy had freed Mrs. Craig's car from the trailing cans, we went home for lunch. Needless to say, Billy was very popular around the church.

On Wednesday afternoon, the first dinner was being prepared. The menu consisted of roast beef, baked potatoes, green beans, and tossed salad, with sweet tea to drink and chocolate cake for dessert. On that first dinner, I think the church lost money on purpose, because later dinners weren't so grand, but the attendance remained high. I guess they wanted to get the people in the habit of coming every Wednesday night, and it worked.

I made several passes through the kitchen. That huge roast smelled so good, but the ladies guarded their food like watchdogs. None of my efforts to sample their wares met with any success; none of my reasons for being in there fooled them for an instant. First I had come into the kitchen with a broom, sweeping close to the freshly cut roast laid in a row of thick, steaming slabs. I casually reached out for the crusty old, savory end piece. My hand was promptly slapped, and I hastily swept myself out of the room.

My second attempt had been more subtle, as I took out the kitchen garbage without so much as a *glance* at the food table in the middle of the room. I returned a moment later with a fresh garbage bag, which I opened with a flourish, placing it in the can. I knew my back was close to the succulent meal; but as I turned, my smile of victory faded when my eyes met the threatening stare of Mrs. Leadbetter. With slumped shoulders, I retreated once again. It seems my reputation had preceded me, along with my protruding stomach, so I gave up and went to polish the brass.

About an hour later, while heading out the back door, I noticed that the kitchen was very quiet. So I peeked in. What I saw surprised me: There was no one there. No mess, no food . . . It actually looked as I had imagined everything until I opened the large refrigerator usually containing butter and bare shelves. It was like opening a treasure chest. It was all there, just waiting for dinner time to arrive. I looked around nervously, expecting them to jump out of their hiding places. But, of course, no one was there except me and the food. Then my conscience showed up and forbade me to take advantage. Well, maybe they won't miss this coarse, but tasty, end slice of roast.

That night, things went well. Mrs. Howell, the church treasurer, had set up a little table and chair with her electric adding machine and worn cigar box. She faithfully collected the price of admission, closely questioning the children to make sure they qualified for the lesser price.

"How old are you? Didn't you have a birthday last month?"

"No, I'm still 11."

"Well, when will you be 12?" she asked little Shelley Debasey.

"On my next birthday," she said, as if it was obvious, and marched on indignantly. Mrs. Howell really enjoyed her position; and as far as I know, she still holds the church's purse strings with an iron grip.

One of the time-honored Baptist traditions is "dinner on the grounds," which goes back to the horse-and-buggy days. The idea is to have a church picnic after the Sunday morning service. The women of the church would warm, unwrap, carry and arrange the food brought from home into a buffet-style dinner on a couple of tables the men had erected and I had covered.

The tables were set up on the west side of the church, for that side was lined with shady pecan trees, carpeted with soft green grass and sweet-smelling clover—the kind that made you wish you could take off your shoes and feel the cool softness between your toes.

Some of those tables were six feet long, and others were eight foot. I remember that type of table at the church from my boyhood. Two of them were really old— so old that they had to have their legs tied into place with a piece of wire or string, for the metal catch hadn't worked in decades. If tied correctly, those old soldiers were as good as the new ones—except for the holes at one end of one of them, which wouldn't show anyway when they were covered, unless someone had the misfortune to place a bowl directly over the hole. In that case, the bowl might then sink slowly until the cover paper tore, with the distinct possibility of the bowl vanishing from sight altogether. The two old tables should have been retired a long time ago, but Baptist churches don't throw anything away, down to the old cigar box in the boiler room labeled "blown fuses." (It actually contained blown fuses which, to my knowledge, are worthless.)

This outdoor feast was Baptist eating at its best—crisp fried chicken, potato salad, green beans, corn on the cob and desserts of all kinds. Pies and cakes were there to be enjoyed along with homemade ice cream. Everyone was feeling the joy and happiness of sharing a good time with one another. Most everyone was smiling and talking, except little Jamie, who was crying since his sister had slapped him right on the mouth for stirring a pitcher of sweet tea with his hand.

Well, I was enjoying myself and eating with real gusto—"seconds" were available as long as the food lasted—when I noticed that Steve Hughes, the new youth director, was sitting at the head of one of those two old tables with its legs tied up. He was really intent on his food and didn't notice when the leg support slipped out of its cradle, leaving the end of the table to be held up by a thin wire and causing his end to lower a little. I guess I should have gone over there and crawled under the table to retie the leg support, but someone might have misunderstood my intentions. In reality, I would have been embarrassed to crawl under the table while everyone was eating, so I let my pride get in the way. Anyway, I just sat where I was, eating a greasy chicken leg, watching Steve with a kind of morbid curiosity.

The funny thing was that, as the wire stretched little by little, Steve's end of the table was slowly drooping. He just kept bending further over his plate, probably thinking of "seconds" himself, apparently unaware of anything being wrong. The other people at that table were oblivious to the situation, as they were deeply engrossed in eating and engaging in joyful conversations. I was just thinking, "Maybe the wire will hold," when wham! the wire snapped and the table fell. Steve was so intent on his food, which had fallen off of his place setting, that he did not notice that everybody else's food, plastic plates and paper cups filled with sweet iced tea were following directly afterward until they slid down on him in one gigantic SLUSH! Everyone was looking at the red-faced man on the ground as if he had willed all their food down on him.

The crowd had mixed responses to the tragedy: Some of us were sympathetic, while others just laughed. Well, I guess the old saying was right: Pride goeth before a fall. My pride had caused that fall, which I could have prevented, and my conscience bothered me for a long time, don't you know. But it had given a whole new meaning to the phrase "dinner on the grounds."

4

CAMPING

P.T. Barnum once said, "There's a sucker born every minute."

I was happy, mainly because that week there were no weddings, dinners, or other social events at the church other than the Sunday and Wednesday night services. For the custodian of a Baptist church, that makes for a quiet week. I looked at my watch: 6:35 p.m., Wednesday, August 7th—two days before the R.A. camping trip. I *used* to love camping: smelling the open fire; watching the gray dawn push away the shadows of the night, bringing the golden sunlight filtering through the tall pine trees; listening to the babbling brook, the singing of the birds; and watching the little squirrels scampering for their breakfast. That's the life—relaxing in the arms of Mother Nature, surrounded by the tranquility that only the woods can provide. It's been a long time since I've enjoyed that kind of peace—too long. I had the excuse I needed.

I climbed the cement steps of the educational building to open the door for my Wednesday night boys group, known as the R.A.s. Our meeting was set opposite the prayer service to give the boys something to keep them occupied and to lend a more tranquil atmosphere to the adult meeting. The honor of being their leader was bestowed upon me just four months ago by unanimous assumption; I remember the day well. I had walked into Brother Johnson's office a bit apprehensively after being summoned into his inner sanctum. The fixed smile upon his face (that same smile he uses in his sermon right before he tells us we are all sinners and are going to hell if we don't repent) made me uneasy.

"Come on in, Dan. Have a seat." He gestured toward an orange imitation-leather chair near his desk. We sat facing each other in the walnut-paneled office. He smiled, rocking back and forth with his elbows on the arms of the chair and his hands folded in front of his face. He looked at me over the tops of his knuckles. In a brief interval of silence, I noticed some dust on the corner of the window ledge, which I had earlier overlooked while cleaning his office, when my attention was drawn back to him as he said, "We need an R.A. chapter in our church."

My gaze dropped from his piercing hazel eyes to the half-empty plastic coffee cup on his cluttered desk. I had the sinking feeling of knowing whom he had in mind for the job.

"Yes," I agreed. "We need someone new in the church who doesn't have a job already . . . Someone young, energetic, with a lot of enthusiasm . . . Someone thin."

Someone who has never met the young boys in question would be even better, I thought to myself.

"Dan?"

"Yes, Brother Johnson?"

"I want you to start our boys' group."

"I'd like to—I really would—but I don't know the first thing about it."

"Dan, were you ever an R.A.?"

"Yes."

"That's good enough for me. You can get all the information and materials you need at the Baptist Bookstore this afternoon. We have an account there."

He leaned forward, shuffled some papers, picked up his pen, and started to write. "Is there anything else, Dan?"

"Why, no. I guess not. I'll be upstairs if you need me." I walked out into the hall in a daze as I thought, *I was only an R.A. for two weeks.*

I came away from the bookstore with an armload of books, banners, pennants, and an R.A. hat for me. The handbook stated that the singlemost influential force in a chapter is the counselor. I was becoming quite excited by the prospect of being a leader to a group of young boys: helping to mold their minds and character, and setting their feet on the straight and narrow path.

My first obstacle to overcome was the recruiting of the

boys. I had found the strongest incentive was a vague promise of a camping trip in the not-so-near future. I ended up with six boys, including my son Billy.

As the weekly meetings progressed, so did the pressure for setting a date for our camping trip. It was finally scheduled for August 9th. The time passed all too quickly.

One week before the date, I contacted Butch Peterson and asked him to come along as our cook and for moral support. Butch weighs about 225 lbs. and stands 6'4". A school teacher, expert camper and outdoor cook, he was also an ex-Marine gunner (the latter being an excellent recommendation in itself). Just to look at him would put "the fear of God" into anyone. Butch also had a large cabin tent that would provide half of our sleeping arrangements. Our other tent was donated by the father of our youngest boy, Calvin, a small but high-spirited youth. The parents seemed almost excited as the boys for the opportunity of this learning experience.

Tonight's meeting would prepare us for the big day tomorrow. I climbed the last few steps, unlocked the door, and switched on the lights. Billy came bounding up the stairs after me, ran into the room, and began to draw spaceships on the blackboard. I had a list of rules ready to go over concerning the etiquette of the woods. Joey, a quiet studious type with thick glasses, was the first to arrive. He was the best behaved of the boys.

"Hi, Billy . . . Mr. Zydiak. I'm all ready for our camp-out."

"That's fine," I replied. "Where are the other boys?"

"I don't know, sir. Ben said he would be here."

Joey and Billy started a game of tic-tac-toe on the board while we waited for the others. Next to come were Barry and Timmy. Barry is tall with curly black hair, thin and has a will of iron. Timmy is the shortest, has sandy blonde hair, is shaped like a bullet, and never says anything, but the others always seem to know what he wants. He usually stands or sits apart from the group, with the four fingers of his right hand in his mouth. They were followed closely by Calvin, the youngest, with a small build, turned-up nose and freckles. His father and I had taken the boys on the only other outing that summer, a fishing trip. The sun was high, no fish had been caught, and I turned to see Calvin walking toward us with his arms at his side calling as he came, "Daddy, get this thing off me." He had cast his line into the water and the hook had ended up in the back of his shirt collar. As he walked toward us, he was dragging his fishing pole behind him.

The next to enter the small meeting room, which on Sunday was a classroom for young adults, was Ben, a chubby ten year old with a baby face. Ben is either going to grow up to be a politician or a gang leader. He has a high degree of leadership quality and can justify any action on his part to the point where a halo seems to shine over his head. I'm reminded of the time we were working on the matchbox racecars you build yourself. Most of the boys had completed their cars and were working on a long piece of plywood for the track. We needed some short screws and Ben was quick to volunteer. After Ben poked Barry in the side, he also volunteered. They left for awhile and came back with the exact size we needed. Later, I discovered the origin of the screws when a door came off in my hand.

Tonight before I came I had called Butch to see how things were progressing.

"Oh, yes, Dan. I just got back from the store. . . . I got everything we'll need, and it only cost me $62.58."

"That's great. Mrs. Craig, our church secretary, will repay you tomorrow."

There were only six boys and two adults, and there were to be only three meals eaten. The finance committee will scream! On the bright side, I thought, *Maybe I won't be asked to head future projects.*

At the end of the meeting, I gave the boys the official announcement: "We'll leave from the church promptly at 4:00 tomorrow afternoon."

By 2:00 the following day, I had the bus full of gas and ready to go. I was wearing my R.A. baseball cap, blue shirt, plaid bermuda shorts, and black tennis shoes. "Yellow Dog," our church bus—so aptly named for its cowardly behavior in traffic—stood under the shade of the huge pecan trees in back of the church. I had my flight glasses on and was ready for anything . . . or so I thought.

Joey and Ben were the first to arrive and were busy stowing their gear in the back of the bus, while I reassured their mothers of the close supervision each child would receive. The rest of the group arrived within the next few minutes. I was quite flattered with the confidence the mothers showed toward me. Some of them didn't even ask what time we would be coming back—if indeed we were even coming back.

It was 5:45 when we finally left the church. I decided this was a good time to find out where we were headed. Butch, being the expert camper, had chosen our campsite.

He had given the address to our church secretary, but had neglected to inform me.

"Where are we headed, Butch?"

"Just past the Atmore State Prison. It's beautiful there, with a lake for swimming and fishing. You can even rent rowboats and play games in their family area."

"Sounds perfect. Do you go there often?"

"No. The last time I got up that way was about two years ago."

Onward we drove to the tune of "99 Bottles of Beer on the Wall," doing the Yellow Dog shuffle due to an imbalance in the wheels.

"Barry, you and Ben put that tent away!"

"But Mr. Zydiak . . . We need to practice putting up a tent," Ben replied.

I looked over at Butch with a pleading look, but Butch just smiled, nodded and said, "It's supposed to be sunny all weekend."

Just at that time, Calvin decided to practice his casting down the center aisle, hooked the back of my cap, and pulled it across Billy's face, which started a free-for-all. Again, I looked to Butch for help, but he just sat with a euphoric look on his face, as he leaned over the front rail watching the trees go by. I knew at that moment that I was on my own.

We arrived at the campgrounds near twilight and parked in a clearing that Butch said would give us easy access to the lake. Butch set up his outdoor kitchen at the rear of the bus and began to prepare our evening meal. I gathered my troop together and proceeded to give a short lecture on survival. About halfway through, Ben asked if we shouldn't be setting up our tents before it got dark. Instantly seeing the logic of this statement, I quickly dismissed them. Having been assured by the older boys of their ability to set up their tent, I left to confer with the cook about supper.

Butch had everything in hand. There was cole slaw, hot dogs, hamburgers with all the fixings, potato chips and other goodies.

"How's everything going?" I asked, a little amazed at his professional preparations.

"Just fine. We'll be ready for supper in about 15 minutes, or as soon as the beans are done."

"That's great."

Everything was going so well, I couldn't believe it; but the night was still young. I went back to see how the boys were doing. I found Billy holding a pole through an eyelet on the outside of the tent, Barry putting poles inside the tent, Calvin hammering down stakes at random, Joey trying to make a hangman's noose out of a piece of rope, and Ben staring at Timmy with a puzzled expression on his face. Timmy had walked up to the tent with his left hand in his mouth and his right hand holding an ax. I quickly disarmed him and gave him a hammer instead.

Soon the tent was ready, and although it leaned a little to the left and was shorter on one side, the boys were very proud of themselves. Everything seemed perfect. The smell of good food wafted through the air, and an evening breeze was picking up. I turned back to congratulate the group, only to find that the gentle breeze had knocked the tent flat. The boys, except for Barry, abandoned the project

36

and started chasing each other. Timmy just stood beside the fallen tent. I asked what was the matter, but to no avail. Ben walked by, hunting for a good flat skipping rock, and said, "He's hungry," without even looking up. Barry worked, Timmy stood, and the other boys played a game of hockey with a tin can.

"Come and get it!" yelled Butch.

The boys, once again except Barry, ran for the food. I tried to persuade him to stop working on the tent until after supper, but he would have none of it. I have always said experience is the best teacher, so I left him to his own devices.

When I joined the others at the back of the bus, I found Butch strangely quiet. For all his preparation and hard work, it seemed all the boys really wanted was a cold hot dog and a stick to roast it with over an open fire. So as not to have any hurt feelings, I ate four hamburgers and three helpings of cole slaw and baked beans, which seemed to make Butch feel better. He ate pretty much the same and washed it down with three cold Cokes from the ice chest.

By the time the meal was over, a tired but triumphant Barry emerged out of the darkness, red-faced with damp hair. "Nothing to it," he said, throwing his arms out to the side. He had found the instructions on the inside flap of the tent. You know what they say, "If all else fails, read the instructions."

After clean-up, I saw Butch bury a half a pot of beans. He reminded me of someone burying their dog. The boys were chasing each other around the campfire and running off all their excess energy. *They're probably tired and can't wait to get to bed,* I thought. Butch had his tent up in five minutes in the dark and had all the sleeping bags unrolled. He left the sleeping arrangements up to me. By the time I had assigned a tent to everyone, Butch was sound asleep. I put three boys in with Butch, and I was to sleep with the rest.

When I arrived in front of the other tent, I found Ben had other plans. He said that, since Calvin's father had donated the tent, Calvin should say who slept in it—the idea being that Ben, Barry, Joey and Calvin would sleep alone. I was to sleep elsewhere.

"There's just one thing you boys have overlooked. Calvin's not in charge—I am."

To this statement, Ben and the others grew quiet, but only for a few seconds. Ben had an inspiration.

"Mr. Zydiak, you want us to gain confidence in our own ability, don't you?"

He was using good logic, and I was tired. I thought about the mattress in Butch's tent and said, "All right, Ben, but you're in charge, and I'm holding you responsible for anything that happens."

"Yes, sir!" came the eager reply from his smiling mouth.

The night was very cool. The sky was clear, revealing a beautiful array of stars. I easily found the Big Dipper, the only constellation I have ever been able to identify.

"Good night, Mr. Zydiak."

"Good night, Ben."

"Good night, Mr. Zydiak."

"Good night, Barry."

"Good night, Mr. Zydiak."

"Good night, John Boy! Would everyone just go to sleep?"

Everyone finally said good night to everyone, except me because I was too tired, Butch because he was asleep, and Timmy because Timmy never says anything.

About 10:00, everything got quiet and I must have dozed off, but was awakened by the sound of running feet. I looked at my watch; it was 12:30. I got up to investigate and found Ben, Barry, Calvin, and Joey running around in the dark. The moon was full, and I could see them darting from tree to tree.

"Ben, come here!"

"We couldn't sleep and . . ."

"Forget it! You and the others march back to that tent and hit the sack."

I turned angrily and went back to my tent. At about 2:30, Ben woke me by shaking my arm. "Mr. Zydiak, we can't sleep. We heard a big wolf right outside our tent. He might come back. If you'll stay with us, we'll go right to sleep."

I thought about his brave talk before bedtime, and then I thought about the promise I had made to his mother. After all, I couldn't let them be eaten by wolves, even if they did deserve it. I left the soft mattress and dragged my sleeping bag across the ground to their tent. I threw my bag on the hard floor and tried to get comfortable. There was an audible sigh of relief from the boys. I was just dozing off again when I heard a scraping sound. It was the noise of sleeping bags being pulled across the floor. Soon I felt the pressure of three warm bodies and sleeping bags against my sides.

I awoke with a start. Everything was dark. Something heavy was laying across my chest. I remembered where I was and soon discovered what the problem was. The tent had fallen; I had to fight my way out. It was 5:30 a.m., and all of the boys were already up. It seems they were playing football and had tripped over one of the ropes, causing the tent to collapse. They decided not to disturb me and left the area rather hurriedly.

Butch was cooking blueberry pancakes, sausage, and toast. Beside him on the table were two gallons of milk and the same of orange juice. The sound and smell of the sausage cooking, combined with the aroma of freshly brewed coffee, quickly aroused my appetite and that of the boys, too. Still half asleep, I took my cup of coffee and was annoyed at the cheerful chatter of the birds. I almost threw a rock at a pesky squirrel foraging for food. Butch, on the other hand, was wide awake and humming to himself.

As I sat drinking my coffee, I got my first good look at our campsite. I got the feeling that it had been longer than two years since Butch had been here. We seemed to be the only humans here. The "beautiful lake" was a wide ditch full of mud and very little water. The "family area with games" was a shed ready to fall over at any given moment. I could see we would have to rely upon nature for our entertainment.

Shortly after breakfast, the boys changed into their swimsuits.

"Where do you think you're going?" I asked.

"Just for a hike, Mr. Zydiak," replied Ben.

"The lake's dried up, except for a few pockets of water too dirty to go in."

40

"We know. We're just going for a walk."

"With swimsuits and towels?"

"It's cooler dressed this way, and we can use the towels to sit on if we get tired," Ben replied without even blinking an eye.

"I don't want you boys in the water."

"No, sir."

"All right. Don't be gone long."

They started off down the dirt trail, yelling and pushing each other. I thought I heard someone say, "Last one in is a rotten egg," but I could have been mistaken. I knew a shortcut to their intended destination, which I had found last night while looking for firewood. When they arrived at the muddy water hole, I was waiting for them.

"Mr. Zydiak, what are you doing . . . I mean how did you . . . ?"

"I just thought I'd take a little stroll, boys."

We all returned to the camp, the boys changed into their jeans, and we went on a real hike, with Butch leading. Our lack of sleep and tired muscles gave way to short tempers.

"CALVIN! If you hook me with that dumb fishing line again, I'll knock your head off!"

I turned around to see what the problem was and saw Calvin trying to get his hook out of the back of Ben's jeans.

Back at the campsite once again, I was resting while Butch cooked fried chicken, mashed potatoes, green beans, and biscuits for lunch. He interrupted my thoughts of a hot bath and a cold drink by saying, "I don't think the ranger would approve of them cutting down those saplings."

"BARRY! BILLY! Bring me those hatchets! Now! Calvin, you and Timmy stop throwing rocks at those baby birds."

After a hearty lunch, we struck our tents and headed for home. The ride back was long and hot. I opened my window and had put out my arm to adjust the mirror, when something grabbed my arm and pulled it over my head. "CALVIN!"

"Sorry, Mr. Zydiak. I think I've got my hook caught in your sleeve."

As the bus entered the church yard, I stopped to take in the scene. There were people everywhere, playing volleyball and socializing. Set up on the grounds were tables laden with food. I had forgotten about our church picnic. Everyone was dressed casually, neat and clean. We were dressed just as casually, but about as clean as a combat patrol who had been out all night on maneuvers.

I drove onto the grounds, and everyone stared as we landed. Needless to say, we were quite conspicuous. We unloaded the gear as fast as we could. All I could think of was getting home. Brother Johnson walked up to me and said, "Thanks for taking the boys. It's good to have y'all back. By the way, we'll be having Baptism in the morning."

"Right . . . I'll take care of it."

Baptism meant having to clean the pool, and then filling and heating it. This process takes about an hour. I turned to go into the church when I felt something jerk at my collar. "CALVIN!"

5

JOLLY ELDERS

I arrived for work at 8:30, coffee in hand, and headed for the kitchen in search of warmth. It was 60º, still cool for the second week in March, even for Mobile. The position of custodian at Springhill Avenue Baptist Church requires patience, understanding, an enormous sense of humor, and above all, flexibility.

"Good morning, Carol," I said.

Carol was the day care cook. She smiled, looked up the clock and then back at me, and said, "It's Jolly Elders' Day."

I have already described my first encounter with the

Jolly Elders and my inaugural trip with Yellow Dog. After that, I found that I had once a month to try and make up for those original mishaps. My church sets aside one day each month for its 35 senior members. Their meeting starts at 10:30 A.M. and is followed by a covered dish lunch at 11:30, or whenever the guest speaker finishes, providing that they have found someone to speak.

The speaker can be anyone from a missionary, home on leave, to a band or choral group. The special guest for the day was a Mrs. Emily Brown, missionary to Japan. She was a small, frail-looking woman dressed in bright blue. She re-minded me of a sparrow darting from group to group of early arrivals in the assembly hall used by these same adults on Sunday morning. I could see them through the open door at one end of the kitchen: women talking, chairs rattling.

I put down my cup and dashed to the dining room. I had forgotten all about it, and nothing was ready. I was greeted by three ladies standing side by side, staring at me. I had the uneasy feeling that they had been waiting for me. I looked around the room and saw that the 10 tables had white, disposable dining paper on them. The silverware was laid out by each place with a folded paper napkin. Bowls of red, pink and white azaleas lined the center of the tables.

"Do you need any help?" I asked as I looked at Mrs. Ellis. She was standing, back straight, looking toward her sister Elizabeth as she answered.

"It appears that we've done everything without your help. Isn't that right, Lizzy?"

"Yes, it does seem that way, Ruth."

The third lady, Mrs. Mulner, smiled and said, "It was

nice of you to ask, though." I knew she was trying to soften the harsh tone used by Mrs. Ellis.

As I backed out of the room (I was reluctant to turn around), I told them I would get a garbage can for their trash.

After I had taken the brown plastic can back to them, I went to the church library. I had seen the jacket of a book I wanted to read on the bulletin board.

I walked in and saw Mrs. Mead sitting behind an enormous, cluttered old desk, repairing the corner of one of the books. Her bright red lipstick was slightly out of line with her mouth, and her wig was a little too far to the right. Her whole appearance gave the impression of a child playing at dress-up.

I looked on the shelves that lined the walls of the musty old room, but was unable to locate the book. I knew of no card catalog, so I asked Mrs. Mead if she knew where to find the book, *Through the Gates of. . . .* I couldn't remember the last word.

"*Through the Gates of Splendor* by Elizabeth Elliott," she said, not looking up from her work.

"You must be clairvoyant," I said. "How do you find what you're looking for?"

"Has nothing to do with clairvoyance. I know my books." She got up and waddled over to the section marked, "Non-Fiction," and scratched her head. Her hair moved slightly forward over her right eye. "It's under "Religion," and has a worn green cover—number 266." After just a few seconds, she had located the book and handed it to me, along with a condensed report of the story.

"It's about the five missionaries who were killed in

Ecuador in 1957. Even though it happened 30 years ago, I still remember hearing it on the radio. The author, Elizabeth Elliot, along with the other wives, finished the work their husbands had started with the very tribe that had killed them."

"Thanks."

"We have some others you might enjoy. How about *Mission to the Headhunters* by Frank and Marie Brown."

"No, this one will be fine."

"How about *In the Clutches of Castro* by Clifton Edgar Fite?"

"No, I don't think so."

"Well, here's *These Strange Ashes* by Elizabeth Elliot."

I had seen the business meeting report for February, and down the column of statistics I spotted the notation, "Library Data . . . Books Checked Out: 6.

When I said immediately, "I'll take them all," she looked very pleased and proceeded to stamp all four books, and I signed the cards each in turn.

After leaving the library, I went outside to wash my buffing pads by hanging them on a fence and spraying them with a hose. I was turning them over when Mr. Niles, a short round man with a splotchy red face, pug nose, and thick glasses, asked: "Dan, could you lead our singing today? My wife usually does it, but I can't find her."

"Well, sure. I guess I can." I turned off the water and followed him inside.

As being one of the few able members of the Jolly Elders, he had assumed leadership and was given due and proper respect from the ladies.

We were standing in the small assembly hall, about to

get things underway, when Mrs. Niles appeared at the back of the room.

"We don't need you now. We've got Dan," Mr. Niles said, pointing at me. She looked relieved and made a hasty exit.

"Attention, please. Dan will lead us in a few songs." He sat down and left me standing behind a shaky wooden podium. We began by singing "Faith of Our Fathers." My loud bass voice drowned out the lower tones of the ladies. Mr. Niles and I were making a joyful noise unto the Lord, or at least a lot of noise.

I was doing some sweeping up after the Jolly Elders had left. It was 3:20 p.m., and I noticed they had left the side door open. I thought nothing of this, as it had happened before. I closed and locked the door. Turning toward the side stairs, I saw a young man dressed in a black tee shirt with a "Jack Daniels" ad on the front. He seemed startled when he saw me.

"May I help you?" I asked.

"No . . . I mean . . . I'm looking for the preacher."

"He's not here right now, but he'll be back soon if you want to wait."

I thought he was probably looking for a handout. I went to the Coke machine, and he followed me. He reached into his jeans pocket and brought out some change. He didn't have enough, so I offered to buy him a Coke.

"Thanks," he said.

We sipped our drinks as I moved across the hall to the boiler room. He followed me again as I began to search for my trash gig. I located the spear-shaped object I was looking for and turned to leave. He dropped his Coke to his side and looked as if he were ready to run. I quickly explained to him that the tool I had was for spearing trash in the church yard. He seemed to relax, and tried to regain his composure. I walked him to the back sidewalk and told him the pastor would be back shortly. I left him there and started my walk around the building. Upon reaching the other side, I noticed the side door was open again. I remembered locking that door just before I met that strange young man. I broke into a run for the door and went up the carpeted stairs two at a time, trash spear in hand. Bursting into the auditorium, I looked around for something missing. There in a line of electrical equipment we use for our sound system was a hole where the recorder had been. I raced back downstairs and out the door. I saw an old black man waiting for the bus.

"Excuse me, sir. Did you see a guy in a black tee shirt carrying something come out of this door?"

"Yes. He got into a car with a girl—waiting for him, I suppose."

"Which way did they go? What kind of car was it? What did the girl look like? Did you get the license number?"

"Well, let me see. It was a little brown car, and dat girl dat was with him was a pretty little thing. I believes they went down there." He pointed down Springhill Avenue, away from town.

"Thanks," I said as I ran for the parking lot, still carrying my spear. In the parking lot, Brother Johnson was just getting out of his car. I told him the details as fast as I could. He never lost his composure.

"Get in," he said. I got in the front and put my spear in the back. I couldn't seem to get rid of the thing.

"There's a pawn shop just up the street," I told him. I felt like this whole thing was my fault. I shouldn't have trusted him. Working in a church had worn down my basic mistrust of people.

The pawn shop turned up nothing. As we were returning to the church, Brother Johnson tried to reassure me it wasn't my fault. I only wish I could have believed him.

I went back into the church, and as I passed a table, I saw the half empty Coke bottle. I couldn't help thinking that we surely lived up to our billing as the friendliest Baptist church in town. Where else do people buy you a Coke right before you rob them?

6

SUNDAY MORNING

The high-domed auditorium darkened into shades of gray from the clouds outside. The huge air conditioner kept the temperature cool in the vast room. The stained-glass windows that lined the sanctuary suddenly came alive as light broke through a cascade of multicolored brilliance, spreading across the walnut pews in a rainbow of color.

It was July, and the temperature was 92º. I headed toward one of my many custodial duties—turning on the air conditioner in our Adult III department. Adult III consists of our senior citizens who have passed the test of time and been found faithful in attendance, year after year. I turned the switch, and nothing happened. I checked the breakers in the boiler room and found nothing wrong. While I pondered this dilemma, I remembered that our pastor, Brother Johnson, had been an electrician before he answered the call to preach. I rushed over to his office to relate the problem to him, thus relieving myself of the responsibility. I walked into the familiar room and noticed a new blue coat slung over one of the orange leather chairs that face his huge, cluttered desk.

Brother Johnson, a slight-built man whose appearance was always neat, had the capability to be in command of any given situation. He was also able to reprimand someone with a kind word, or simply by the way he looked at them.

"It's the air in Adult III," I said as he returned thoughtfully to his desk.

"What?"

"The air conditioning in Adult III won't come on. I checked the breakers, and nothing . . . I mean, they're working, so it must be something else."

"The electrician was supposed to have fixed that last week. Come on. Let's take a look and see what can be done."

We adjourned to the boiler room, so named because it housed the water heater, the plumbing for most of the church, and two walls of electrical boxes. After a few minutes of examination, he discovered the problem. The church had had the old fuse box updated to a breaker system, and the electrician had failed to connect the wire leading into the unit. As Brother Johnson rolled up his sleeves, getting ready to tackle the job, I stood by helplessly.

It seemed that when the thick stiff wires were in place, the nut that held them would drop to the floor; and when the nut was on, the cable would drop out. As time passed on, the wires became snarled.

"Can I get you a pair of pliers?"

"No, I've almost got it."

"There's a pair in the office."

"I don't think I need them."

After 15 minutes of watching him work in the heat, I was sweating; but apart from his hands being dirty, he showed no signs of being affected.

"I'll be right back," I said as I headed for the office. He made no reply. I returned to the back door of the old building, pliers in hand, as the door swung open. We faced each other for an instant with no words exchanged, but I knew he was going for the pliers. I gave them to him as we shared a smile, and he said, "Thanks." The wiring took another 10 minutes of his working and my sweating. I learned a lesson in perseverance and commitment from that experience. I wish the day had ended there . . . .

The early arrivals were already there, and I was behind in my schedule of unlocking doors and gates. The service was about to begin, so I went up to the sunlit auditorium and took a back row seat, only to notice that the water level in the baptismal pool, which was located behind the choir, had dropped about five inches. Brother Johnson likes the water near the top of the glass, but I remembered the last time I had filled it that high. Mark Prichette was being baptized and had been told not to lock his knees, but Mark forgot or got scared, and when he went under, his legs surfaced, and he scissor-kicked water all over the back row of the choir. It was rather amusing to watch as those somber men casually wiped water from their heads and faces, never turning, but looking straight ahead with water-spotted robes.

I decided to try and raise the water level, but not with the rust-filled plumbing—it would only let mud in. I got a garden hose and draped one end over my shoulder and crimped the hose. Then I raced up the back stairs, charging up the last flight of stairs to the men's dressing room. Upon entering, hose in hand, I faced a startled Brother Johnson and two other men dressed in the traditional white gowns. Not knowing if this was part of the usual ceremony, they looked to the pastor for reassurance. Brother Johnson, ever calm, asked, "Dan, what are you doing?"

"The water level dropped. Probably the drain was leaking or something. I thought I would just . . ."

"—It's too late now; we'll have to make do with what we have."

Backing up, I tripped over the hose; and as I put out my hand to keep from falling, I accidentally let go of the crimp in the hose. After the initial shock, I slowly backed out of the room, leaving the three of them nodding and smiling...and dripping wet. I shamefacedly dragged the hose back down the stairs.

Moments later, as I rolled the hose into a neat coil, thinking about the disappointed look on my pastor's face, old John Dogooder came by and said, "What ya doing, Dan? Killing some time?"

"Just rolling up the hose, John." I wished I could have turned the hose on him.

Part of our morning service is welcoming the visitors. While the choir sings, we stand and greet each other. It was during this part of the service that I regained my peace, only to quickly lose it again. I saw Mrs. Crowley making her way toward me, smiling with outstretched arms. *How sweet,* I thought as I bent forward to greet her. As she hugged my neck, she whispered in my ear, "The toilet in the ladies room is overflowing." I drew back as she smiled and said, "Just thought you'd like to know." She hurried on to greet some other poor, unsuspecting soul.

After unstopping the toilet, I was returning the plunger to the boiler room when I passed John Dogooder, who said, "Shouldn't you be in church?" I smiled my best plastic smile and continued on.

I decided to save myself some time and open the baptismal drain while I was in the boiler room. I didn't think anyone would notice, since it drained slowly and would only lower a couple of inches by the time church was over. I returned upstairs just as the service was concluding, and upon the last "Amen," the organ began to play, the choir began to sing, and the baptismal pool began to gurgle. Something had gotten caught in the drain. Not to be out-done, the organist, with a determined look on her face, played louder. The surprised choir director frowned at the organist and then back at the choir, rolled her eyes heaven-ward as if asking for divine guidance, and directed them to sing louder. The singing came to an end, the music faded away, and the organist sat with a triumphant smile upon her face that quickly turned sour as the drain made a final slurp and sucked the obstruction through the pipe.

On my way out, a little blue-haired lady waddled up to

me and said, "There are toilet paper rolls in the men's bathroom window, and it doesn't look very nice."

"I'll take care of it," I said as I wondered why she was looking in the men's bathroom window.

Outside, as I shook Brother Johnson's hand I said, "I'm sorry for all the distractions."

He just grinned and asked, "What distractions?"

We exchanged understanding smiles, and I felt better as I closed and locked the doors.

7

THE WEDDING

Sunlight is shining through the branches of the old oak trees that line Springhill Avenue. I am sweeping wedding rice from the sidewalk in front of the church. Off to my left are a half-dozen sparrows feasting on the fallen rice. It amuses me to think of all the people in fine clothes who, driving their big new cars and eating rich food, are unaware that the birds struggling to survive would benefit from the union of these two young people.

I started out this week as usual, by checking with Mrs. Craig, our church secretary, to see what the week's activities were. I walked into the small, well-lit office adorned with its

56

black leather furniture and artificial plants. To the right, sat the secretary. She is wearing her favorite red blouse with a string tie at the neck. Her blue-gray hair is neat as usual. She has a standing appointment at the beauty parlor every week, although I can never see any difference before or after. She motioned for me to wait for her to hang up the phone. I slouched into the work room, helped myself to a cup of her coffee, then returned to find Mrs. Craig sitting back in her swivel chair, also sipping coffee.

Rolling her eyes heavenward, she groaned, "There's to be a wedding come Friday night, and a rehearsal with dinner, Thursday. That was the bride's mother on the phone." She took another sip before continuing. "Said she'd contact you later. Her number's unlisted. Oh, yeah . . . the dinner's being catered."

"Who's getting married?"

"Martha Elders and Bruce Martin."

"That doesn't ring a bell with me."

"Probably wouldn't. They haven't been to church in years. I can't understand why they want a church wedding when they don't attend church."

As Mrs. Craig's voice grew louder, her face became suffused with color. I knew I had found one of her pet peeves. It wasn't long before I was out of the office and busy with my regular routine.

As I walked into the auditorium to polish the brass plates on the doors, I noticed a strange little man in a blue suede coat holding a pad and pencil. I introduced myself, and he said he was "John, the florist," and asked me about the pulpit furniture, which consists of five heavy wooden chairs, a thick ornate table, and the pulpit itself. He wanted to know who was to move the furniture. I told him the ushers were responsible for it and usually moved it during the rehearsal.

"Wouldn't it be lovely if they didn't have to bother with that . . . if all of this could be moved by this afternoon?" His upturned palms and feminine voice told me whom he had in mind for the job.

"Yes, that would be very nice, and I hope you find someone to do it," I replied, making a hasty retreat.

The week was progressing well, except for the fact that I hadn't heard from Mrs. Elders, and it was Thursday. I set up our small dining hall with tables and chairs for 25 people. I decided not to put paper on the tables due to the fact that the dinner was being catered.

Contrary to what people might think, I like weddings. It's not because I get all choked up seeing two people starting a life together—although I like to think that in a small way, my efforts have contributed to their union. But alas, I am quite mercenary, and the fact that I get paid (preferably in cash) from the bride's mother is my primary joy of the occasion.

At 5:45 p.m., I was out in the parking lot making sure the parking signs were in the right place, when I noticed someone coming. A petite blonde of about 18 was getting out of an old blue Ford and walking toward me. Judging from her clothes (blue jeans and a tee shirt), I figured she was probably not here for the rehearsal but was lost and wanted directions.

"May I help you?" I asked.

"Yes. I'm Mary Lou Fowler, and I'm looking for Mrs. Elders."

"So am I. What time is the rehearsal?"

"Mrs. Elders told me to be here no later than 5:45, and here I am," she said, holding her arms out for emphasis.

"So I see, and right on time," I said, looking at my watch.

"She probably told me 5:45 because I'm always late."

Sure enough, Mary Lou was right, for Mrs. Elders, her daughter, and the rest of the wedding party didn't show up until 6:15. The rehearsal was to start at 6:30.

I immediately attached myself to Mrs. Elders, a tall, stout, loud woman who could have been a rodeo star—probably in bull riding. I needed to extract information to better prepare and possibly get paid early. This whole thing was beginning to take on a fly-by-night appearance.

Mrs. Elders was talking a mile a minute and not really saying anything. I supposed she was just nervous and didn't realize how obnoxious she was becoming.

Turning abruptly, she faced me with hands on hips and head tilted to one side, asking, "Do you have any idea how much this thing is costing me? Well, of course I can afford it, but that's not the point. I mean the whole thing is so expensive. The reception alone will cost . . . well . . . you just have no idea. Ever since Harold left me, I've had to raise that child by myself. Even though her father sends money and pays the bills every week, he hasn't been tied down like I have." She hesitated as if looking for sympathy. "Well, all that will change after tomorrow night."

I used this pause in our one-sided conversation to take control. "You know, the day of the wedding is so hectic that I usually get paid at the rehearsal."

She merely smiled, looked at me for a moment, and said, "See me at the dinner tonight. You are going to stay, aren't you?"

"Yes, I will be here."

Everyone at the rehearsal, except for the prospective couples' mothers, were dressed more for a football game than a wedding rehearsal. The young girls were wearing jeans and tee shirts, and the young men wore pretty much the same. Most of the party were wearing boots and Western belt buckles.

As I was standing in the auditorium with the wedding party, a woman entered through the double doors in the back of the room. It was Mrs. Martin, the groom's mother. She was a tall, skinny, scarecrow of a woman with black hair. Her cheekbones, accentuated by two bright red balls of color, brought attention to her too pale complexion and sunken cheeks. Her lips were coated with a think red lipstick that only added to her Halloween appearance.

I asked Mrs. Martin what time the caterer would be arriving.

She looked surprised as she replied, "Caterer? What caterer? I'm not paying good money for a dinner I can cook myself. Now don't worry about a thing—I'll handle everything."

After the rehearsal, the wedding party went downstairs to eat and I stayed behind to turn off the auditorium lights.

When I went into the dining room, I was a little surprised to see they hadn't used any tablecloths. The food was laid out buffet-style.

Brother Johnson was just entering the dining room. He took one look at the food and excused himself, saying he had a previous engagement. As I approached the table, I could see why: The egg salad and tuna sandwiches were dry and hard. Further down were toothpicks stuck in squares of cheese and some potato salad that was more mayonnaise than potato. At the end of the table was the beverage section, with a choice of Coke or Sprite, in two-liter bottles. Next was an ice chest full of melting ice, the idea being to scoop up ice in your hand or cup and somehow gracefully pour from the bottles. I managed this feat and took a seat next to Mrs. Elders.

As I was trying to choke down a sandwich, I turned and found Mrs. Elders staring at me with a strange expression on her face.

"Where's Brother Johnson?"

"I believe he had a previous engagement," I replied politely.

"Well, he don't know what he's missing."

I thought to myself, *Oh yes, he does,* but I smiled at Mrs. Elders and said, "He sure is missing a fine meal."

She looked proud even though she had had no part in the food preparation.

"Are you sure you have had enough to eat?" Mrs. Elders inquired. "There's plenty more where that came from."

Surely enough, there was. Everyone was eating light, including myself. "I'm not very hungry. This is fine, thank you."

All the time I had sat there, she had not mentioned paying me. I remained quiet and amused myself by watching people eat and by thinking this was more like an indoor picnic than a sit-down dinner.

The bride-to-be, Martha Elders, was 5'7" and had soft brown, shoulder-length hair, a slim, petite build, and a face that seemed to have the innocence of a much younger girl. She was talking and hanging on the arm of her fiancé.

As the young guests finished their meal, they began to drift out in pairs, on to more rewarding activities. After all, they were young and so was the evening.

Only the two mothers and I remained. Mrs. Elders assured me they wouldn't leave a mess for me to clean up, and they didn't. I had a garbage can ready for their use; but to my surprise, only paper plates and napkins were thrown away. I supposed they were saving the rest for some future social event.

Mrs. Elders was preparing to depart, so I decided to be aggressive. Hadn't I sat through that horrible meal as requested? "Mrs. Elders, do you have a check for me?" Her reply caught me off guard.

"Tomorrow . . . Tomorrow at the wedding. Don't worry: I won't forget you," and she walked away.

Friday afternoon, as I was walking through the kitchen that leads into the reception area, I met Mrs. Jones, the lady in charge of decorations and food preparation. She is a short, plump lady whom I enjoy working with. I noticed a new garbage can standing at the end of the kitchen table and thought, *At least Mrs. Jones is making some attempt at professionalism; she brings her own equipment for clean up.* I felt a lot better about things, having her on the team.

"Ah, Mrs. Jones. I see you have things well in hand," I said as I entered the reception hall.

"Well, to tell you the truth, things are running a little rough. My car's air conditioner broke, and I was afraid the Crisco in the icing would melt and ruin the cake."

I hadn't realized that thick white icing I had enjoyed all

these years was half Crisco. I told her the cake looked fine. I began to think, *I want my money, and I want to go home.*

The groom, Bruce Martin, was 5'7", had blonde, curly hair, a round face, and a quiet manner about him.

Bruce, his mother, and his father arrived first. This was the first time I had ever seen an all-white tuxedo. I told him he looked great. He seemed quite nervous, and when Mary Lou came up to me and asked if I had seen Martha or her mother, stressing that it was only 20 minutes until the wedding, Bruce seemed to fall apart before my eyes.

Suddenly, the back door opened, and one of the bridesmaids said, "She's here."

Mrs. Elders entered, daughter in tow. Martha seemed relaxed, unlike her flustered mother. They whisked by me and disappeared into the dressing room. The mother emerged a few minutes later and appeared to avoid me.

Moments before the ceremony was to begin, the bride appeared in a long, white lacy grown. She looked truly beautiful with her face all aglow with anticipation. She seemed to float by me to take her place at the back of the auditorium. I hurried to take a back row seat.

I was seated behind two elderly ladies. "I just love candlelight services," one of the ladies said. The other replied with a nod of her head. I, on the other hand, was thinking, *How in the world am I ever going to take care of the wax that is dripping on to the carpet?*

As the organ began to play, the flower girl was throwing paper flower petals. The same lady commented, "Oh, how lovely." I'm thinking, *Thousands of those little lovelies to clean up.*

The ceremony went as smooth as the Crisco icing on the cake downstairs.

As the service was coming to a close, I made a hasty retreat and went downstairs to see if Mrs. Jones needed my help. I found her in the kitchen, mixing up about 15 gallons of punch in the garbage can I had seen earlier. I was a little surprised, but said, "You seem to have a good supply of punch," while thinking, *I probably won't have any cake or punch, even though I know the brown garbage can is new.* I do have to give her credit, though: she served the punch from an elegant punch bowl.

The guests were coming down now and moving toward the receiving line to congratulate the young couple. Everyone seemed to be having a good time eating Crisco cake and drinking garbage can punch.

Near the end of the reception, the guests gathered around the couple as the groom knelt before his new bride to remove her garter. Though red in the face, he was finally able to complete his quest and was greeted with applause and cheers.

While the bride retired to the dressing room to change, her mother marched up to me, handed me an envelope, and said, "Thank you for your help." Inside was a simple note that read, "Thank you for your efforts. Included is a small token of our appreciation."

The announcement was made that the time had come for the bride and groom to depart. As the wedding guests were gathering handfuls of rice, the new couple took their place in the foyer. While waiting for the signal to leave, I wished them good luck and shook the groom's hand. Before they turned to go, the bride came over to me and hugged my neck and whispered in my ear, "Thank you." At that moment, I realized that her "Thank you" had meant more to me than the fee I had received from Mrs. Elders.

8

THE FUNERAL

The day was warm for April—a spring vacation of sorts from my custodial work. But this wasn't supposed to be fun. We were seated under a green canopy. The brown metal folding chairs that faced the grave were filled with my mother's family, who had come to pay their last respects to my grandmother.

My brother Bobby and I, along with six of our cousins, were to be pallbearers. All of them lived in Virginia except Topper, who was home from M.I.T. He was the family genius. Tall with shoulder-length brown hair and pale blue eyes, his expression was always one of calm acceptance.

Seated next to Topper were Tom and Joey, quiet boys who had never displayed a lot of smarts. Once, when we were playing "Hide and Seek," Tom had come into a room where we were hiding and asked, "Is anyone in here?" Cousin David couldn't resist yelling from the closet, "No. We're outside." Tom went outside to find us.

Thinking back on that funeral service brings tears to my eyes—not tears of sadness, although I missed my grandmother terribly, but tears of hysteria. Eric and Topper were to be on the ends of the casket. Phil, Bobby, and I were to be on one side with David on the other, flanked by Tom and Joey. As we neared the hearse, Tom dropped off, and Joey followed suit. David was left trying to hold up his half of the coffin alone. He was looking over his shoulder trying to get Tom and Joey's attention, to no avail. They were standing with their heads bowed and hands folded behind their backs. Tom was wiping away an imaginary tear from his eye. It was really quite touching. As David looked to us for help, what he saw was discouraging. We had begun a subdued laughter, which resembled crying due to the tears that were gathering in our eyes. I heard one of my aunts comment, "God bless 'em: them boys sure loved their grandmother." This revelation brought on renewed laughter and tears bordering on hysteria. As the coffin teetered back and forth on David's shaky legs, Topper stepped back to the end of the coffin to help balance it. After depositing the casket safely, we retreated to the waiting cars to proceed to the cemetery, handkerchiefs to our faces to muffle the laughter that was taken for grief.

Someone had thought it would be all right for the five of us—Phil, David, Eric, Bobby, and me—to ride together to the cemetery in Phil's car. Phil owned a red Chevrolet "Impala," complete with racing cam. The jumping red car took its place in line with the somber black ones.

"Those two morons almost made us drop Grandma in the gutter," said David.

"It's okay," said Phil. "We didn't drop her. As for Frick and Frack, what did you expect? I just hope they don't screw up at the cemetery."

"Can't you just see the paper tomorrow?" Bobby asked. "Mrs. Vetra S. Jones was dumped in her grave Saturday as Tom and Joey, her loving but moronic grandsons, let her go...near the hole."

"Phil . . . Hey, Phil! Where you going? I been trying to call you all day," said a boy on the sidewalk, walking as fast as we were driving.

"I'm going to bury my grandmother. I'll see you later at the club!" he yelled back.

The rest of the trip to the cemetery was uneventful, and as we sat in those cold chairs staring at the flower-covered coffin, my mind drifted back to the happier times I had spent at my grandmother's. We called it "Memaw's Mountain" because her house was nestled at the base of a mountain with a stream running on two sides. About 20 feet from her back door was a swinging bridge that led to a winding mountain trail. To the left of the trail was a steep gravel slant that we called "Phil's Fire Trail," so named because Phil decided to slide down that 20-foot slope, and the friction nearly set his pants on fire.

To the right of her house was a 12-foot dam. At times, I would cross it to go mountain climbing. I never used the usual gear one would suppose a climber needed. All I had was a pair of Keds tennis shoes to see me through. The dangerous part was about 40 feet up, where there were not too many jutting rocks to hold on to—just loose gravel and hearty shrubs. Hearty shrubs have saved my life many a time. I began to believe in predestination, hanging on to the face of that cliff, while my feet scratched off on loose gravel and my hearty shrub began to come out by the roots. Just as I thought I was going to die, I saw another hearty shrub and grabbed for it in desperation. It held. I knew I couldn't give up then, for there was another hearty shrub to the left and so on, until I reached the top.

Around the front of the house was a battleship gray wooden porch with a swing. In the front yard were about 50 giant spruce trees, which surrounded the porch like a privacy fence. An old green glider was in the left half of the grassy circle. Sometimes, when I would get worn out from swimming or playing with my cousins, I would lie on the glider and close my eyes. I could hear bees buzzing close by, mingled with the sound of the water rushing over the dam. At those moments, all the world seemed right with me.

Directly in front of the porch and through the trees was a gravel road that followed the stream to the highway. We would make a daily pilgrimage to the row of rusty mailboxes, to the one marked, "Vetra S. Jones." I never knew why, but we didn't wear shoes for this task, and the rocks always hurt my feet.

We had arrived at my Uncle Al's at 10:00 the day before the funeral. My sister Marcia took charge while our parents were at the funeral home. The combination of a sleepless night and being united with the Jones boys was positively intoxicating. We were laughing and joking until Marcia grabbed my arm and dragged me into a nearby bedroom. She jerked me around, and fire was coming out of her eyes. My smile quickly faded.

"Don't you know why we're here?" she snapped. "Daniel Zydiak, you just remember who you are. You're not one of those Jones boys, and you're not going to act like one."

Yes, but . . ."

"—You should just be glad our father isn't here to see you."

"What's that supposed to mean? I've just spent the night riding up here with your husband, and I'm a little tired—that's all."

That made sense to her, but Zydiaks never apologize to each other, so she said a little softer, "Just remember what I said."

They lowered the casket into the ground, and it was over. The next day I would be returning home; but for a few brief hours, all the fun of my youth had returned to me, and I don't think Memaw would have minded at all.

9

TENT REVIVAL

Revival in a Baptist church occurs about twice a year with a lot of planning and promotion. One of the reasons we have these services is to save souls. Also, due to the routine of the church, we as Christians sometimes get so relaxed in the mechanics of our religion that we lose the excitement of first becoming a Christian. For instance, you go to Sunday School and the morning worship service, and during the sermon, the pastor says something that hits home, and you think, "I'm going to change."

After Sunday dinner, you watch the game on television, take a nap, and go back to church that night, and for some reason, because you go to church every time the doors are open, you feel pretty good about yourself. However, at times we may catch ourselves growing complacent—that's where revival comes in. After you go to revival meeting every night for two weeks, you're a new man, a better man, filled with virtue and the love of Jesus.

I remember once, when I was a young boy, we had a visiting preacher at church. My sister Marcia was sitting with some of her teenage friends close to the front of the auditorium. I was several rows back, next to my father. The young preacher was trying to drive home his point that all have sinned, so he asked the audience if there was anyone present who had never sinned. My father, who is a good man but also a practical joker, raised his hand. This caught the preacher completely off guard, so he stammered, "Well, with one exception, we know that all have sinned." As he said that, everybody in the church turned to look at Dad, who sat there with a serene look of innocence upon his face. As I looked around at everybody looking at us, I felt proud to have such a good father. Everyone looked, except for my sister Marcia. I could see the back of her head slide out of view, on her way to hide under the pew.

I can remember one time the church decided to have an old-fashioned tent revival. I don't know where they got the big circus-like tent, but they set it up in the yard next to the church, and added sawdust and folding chairs. This was a cracker jack idea, except it was held in August, which, as y'all know, on the gulf coast is like a steamship's boiler room—high humidity, high temperatures, and hot nights. You know the kind of nights—when everyone's neck and face are glistening. In this particular service, the choir director announced that we were going to sing "Standing on the Promises." "Now," he said, "you can't sing 'Standing on the Promises' while sitting on the premises, so let's all stand again."

Well, right away, you start to dislike the music director. First off, it's hot, and he's practically got us doing calisthenics. Eventually, the evangelist starts preaching about sin and repentance, and it's so hot you can't tell who's under conviction because everyone is sweating. In spite of the funeral parlor fans—so-called because a local funeral home had an advertisement on the back—it was still sweltering. The sermon continued in spite of the traffic noise of Spring Hill Avenue only a few yards away.

Looking down at the sawdust, I started to make a little pile of the stuff between my shoes, as if playing with sand at the beach. Glancing across the aisle, I saw that a little girl had gotten a similar idea, slipped out of her chair, and was using her hands to make a sawdust castle.

Her mother was cradling her little brother's head, who was fast asleep. That little boy sleeping in his mother's arms reminded me of resting in the peace that Jesus can provide.

It was close to the end of the service, and one older woman named Paula started to snore loudly. Well, someone sitting next to her tried to wake her with an elbow, but with disastrous results. At first, she started grunting in short, fast gulps. At that moment, as the preacher was saying, "If any here be in sin, let him come to the Lord," Paula started talking loudly in her sleep, "What? What did he say?"

An older lady behind her said, "If you're in sin, you

should come to the Lord, deary." As the laugher subsided, the quick-witted evangelist said, "Now that we've cleared that up, if there is anyone here that is unsure of his or her salvation, please come forward."

On the second night of the revival, I decided to use my resourcefulness by going to the third floor of the old building, where I remembered seeing two huge old oscillating fans, each mounted on a two-inch stainless steel pipe, which was six feet long with a large weighted base that looked like a 100-pound weight. Finding them was no problem; getting them down was. I tilted the fan and motor back, and managed to walk it to the top of the stairs. The idea was to lower it one step at a time, and then go back and get the second one.

I got the first fan down the first three stairs as planned, but on the fourth, I got in a hurry. I lost control of the heavy monstrosity when the fan tipped forward and the base started sliding down the stairs. I knew it would tumble if I didn't do something, so I jumped on the end of the base and grabbed the pole about six inches below the fan and tried to pull back. But all I was able to do was to tilt the already moving base back a little. So down the stairs I went—bump . . . bump . . . bump—in rapid order, all the way down to the next landing. I must have looked like I was trying to invent a new sport, something akin to wind surfing.

When the shock wore off, I felt relieved that neither the fan, nor I, had been damaged. After getting both fans down and into the large tent without any further excitement, I found ample extension cord and was ready to surprise everyone that night with a cooler tent. When the time came and everyone was seated, I turned on the big blowers and they worked fine, cooling the tent at first. I could hear an audible sigh of relief, which made me swell with pride and think all the trouble had been worth it.

When the motors reached their top RPMs, however, the sawdust started to fly. For a while, it looked like a sand storm in the tent. I quickly turned off the wind machines, and with a red face, tried to become invisible. Actually, the blowing sand seemed to add to the sermon that night, which was entitled, "Wandering in the Wilderness."

After the service, I saw a couple of little old ladies with white dustballs in their tousled blue-gray hair that made it look like they had been to a fight instead of church, and their expressions looked like they were looking for one. Needless to say, we never had another old-fashioned tent meeting.

10

Day Care

Like many Baptist churches, we have a day care program. It all started with the realization that the Sunday School rooms were only being used on Sunday and Wednesday nights. The fact that church space was virtually unused most of the time was close to waste—and that's one thing Baptists can't tolerate. Also, a church day care would help the community by providing a safe place in which working mothers could leave their children and know they would be well cared for.

It was Mrs. Rachel Banks who approached the pastor with the idea of starting a day care at Spring Hill Avenue

Baptist, and I have to say in her behalf that she worked very hard, teaching the five-year-olds herself for the first year, in addition to overseeing the administration, and organizing and promoting it without pay until the day care was strong enough to support itself. Even then, she was frugal with the day care account. She deserved her reputation for being a "penny pincher," always seeking ways to save money.

Of course, the day care account was listed in the church's monthly business report, which was revealed at the meeting held on the first Wednesday night of every month. At first, the membership was just glad the day care was not "in the red," and therefore not an added burden on the church. But as time passed and the account continued to grow, people began to take notice of the fine job Mrs. Banks had done. Pretty soon, there was $5,000 . . . then $10,000 . . . and finally $20,000 in the account. The pastor praised Mrs. Banks' efforts from the pulpit, and she was content in the knowledge that her efforts were helping the church, and that all did not go unnoticed by her peers.

Sometimes, working around the day care would lend itself to funny situations, like the time I was mopping up a Kool Aid spill in the hall of their building. A little girl walked out of the bathroom and said, "Mr. Dan, how old are you?"

"Four," I replied, teasing her.

"That's great—we'll be in the same class next year!" she said happily, walking down the hall to her class.

Another time, my wife was opening the day care for a few days, to help out as the usual "opener" was on vacation.

This required her to be there before 6 A.M. As it was dark at that time of the morning, she requested that I accompany her for safety and companionship. I was not a willing participant in this venture, since normally we didn't have to go to work at the church until eight. I was there, but not enjoying it, and I looked it. Sour faced and in bad humor, I longed to be back in bed, but knew that wasn't going to happen. So, there I stood, ready to answer the ring of the fire alarm-like door bell, as the door was kept locked until daylight. The bell rang at 5:50 A.M.; it was little Jimmy and his mother, whom I had never seen before. I must have looked pretty sinister, for after Jimmy was settled in with some cereal, my wife Gayle walked Mrs. Lee to the door, and as she was leaving, she turned to Gayle and whispered, "Is he holding a gun on you? Do you want me to call the police?"

"No, I don't think so—he's my husband," she whispered back, trying to suppress a smile. Well, it's nice to make a good impression on people.

It's been said that children say the darndest things, and I can vouch for that. One time, my wife was trying to teach her class about Adam and Eve. She held up an artist's picture of the garden of Eden, displaying lots of vegetation and animals, including lions and elephants, and featuring a naked man and woman discreetly standing behind adequate foliage. "Can anyone tell me who God created first?" Gayle asked the class.

After thinking about it, one little boy said, "Oh yeah, that's Tarzan, and that's Jane." He smiled broadly, proud of himself.

On another occasion, Mrs. Patty, who taught the four-year-old class, was sitting out in the play yard in a folding chair, her back to the fence, keeping watch over her students on a hot afternoon, when one of her girls ran up with her hands clutching her throat.

"What's wrong, Kathy?" she asked in a sympathetic tone.

"Miss Patty, my neck's leaking," replied the grief-stricken child.

After prying the child's dirty fingers away, a sweaty neck was revealed. After a hug of reassurance and a wipe from a small ever-present towel, she sent the child back to play.

When you think about it, you drink water, and it goes through your neck on the way to your stomach. So, to discover water on the outside of your neck, it would seem logical to conclude that your neck was leaking. How many times does the devil come to us with needless worry?

On one particular November near Thanksgiving, Mrs. Banks had arranged to have the children visit a local nursing home to spread joy to the elderly. I was replacing fluorescent bulbs in the hall when Mrs. Banks asked me to come into one of the classrooms. I had no idea what she wanted, but followed her into the room. The children and teacher were out in the play yard. The room was furnished with short rectangular tables of blond wood with matching stout little chairs. Mrs. Banks sat at one of the tables in a tiny chair and waved me over to one near her. It felt odd sitting in a chair that was six inches high. Here we were, two adults, feet on the floor, knees higher than our waists, having a serious conversation.

Mrs. Banks scooted her chair forward, leaned toward me, and motioned me closer. As I leaned nearer to her, she said, "Dan, I need your help. We are visiting the Willows Home for the Elderly, and I need you to drive us in the bus. I'm sorry for not giving you more notice, but with all the preparations, I forgot."

"No problem," I said, glad for a chance to do something different. "I'll just put the bulbs and ladder away, and I'll be ready."

"That's good, because I'm really counting on you," she said. "Oh, by the way, we're going as pilgrims and Indians, and I'm short of Indians, so I want you to go as the chief."

While the thought sank in, she added that she had made a costume for me. I just sat there in shock, saying to myself, *I just agreed to drive the bus for a change of pace.* I said to her, "Maybe I should just stay with the bus while we are there."

"No, that won't be necessary, and as I've already told you, I need you to lead the Indians in like you're doing a war dance," she said, and got up easily from the little chair. As I struggled to regain my feet, she slipped a brown construction paper headband on my head, which was surrounded with all different colored construction paper feathers. As I stood up, she was fitting me with a brown paper grocery bag vest. The two bags had been cut open and stitched together with pink yarn, with the store logos on the inside. The vest was decorated with many colors and had construction paper fringe glued on the breasts. I went to the church office frowning in my paper Indian costume, my feathers waving independently. As I sought the key to the bus, Mrs. Craig said, "How! Big chief go on raid to old folks home."

"Pale face squaw not tease big chief if want to keep scalp," was all I could come up with as I left the office with the key.

Well, there we were: a bus full of pilgrims and Indians. Mrs. Banks dressed as a pilgrim and me as an Indian, and everybody was singing, "Little bunny fufu, we don't want to see you picking up the field mice and bopping them on the head." Everyone sang except me because I was driving and sweating, and didn't want to sing. As we proceeded, my headband feathers got wet at the bottoms, which made them droop like wilted flowers all the way around my head, so that I now looked more like a court jester than an Indian.

When we finally got off the bus at the nursing home, Mrs. Banks handed us each a small paper basket containing candy to give to the elderly patients and told the children dressed as Indians to follow me as we danced in.

"Baptists don't dance!" I protested.

"Oh come on, be a good sport; we're going to have ice cream later," she entreated and led the pilgrims in a kind of march. I swallowed my pride, bent over slightly, and hopped and skipped through the door, whooping like they do in movies about Indians. As I hopped and pranced before the audience of elderly people sitting in a sort of living room, I thought, *At least we'll have ice cream later.*

The program consisted of Mrs. Banks leading the children in some songs I didn't know and handing out the candy and stuff to the elderly. It was at this time that the conversation got a little weird.

"Are you a real Indian?" asked one short lady.

"No, I'm the bus driver," I said, trying to settle the matter.

"Well, you don't look like any bus driver I ever saw," said a tall lady.

"Do you have a bus driver costume?" asked the short lady.

"No, I don't have a bus driver costume; I only agreed to wear this Indian thing just this once," I retorted.

"Well, do you have a bus driver's hat? My Fred was a bus driver, and he had a whole uniform," mentioned the short lady.

"No, I'm the church custodian who drives the bus for the day care occasionally," I explained.

"Well, I wish you would make up your mind: first you're an Indian, then you're a bus driver, and now you tell us you're a custodian," said the tall lady.

"I'm an Indian," I said, just to end the discussion. "I've got to go now. It's been nice talking to you," I said.

"He seems like such a nice young man," said the short lady as I turned away.

"But he seems so confused," observed the tall lady as I walked out of earshot.

Later, Mrs. Banks thanked me with a Dixie cup of ice cream, and it tasted delicious.

On another occasion close to Thanksgiving, Gayle was teaching her class about sharing and the first Thanksgiving. She held up an artist's picture of pilgrims and Indians eating together at a large table. She asked if anyone knew why the pilgrims had invited the Indians to dinner.

After the usual pause, one little fellow said, "Yeah, first you need to feed them, and then you kill them!"

Before Gayle could react, another boy added, "The

only good Indian is a dead Indian!" followed by a general agreement of the class in "Hu ha" and "Yeah!"

After Gayle had quieted the lynch mob, she tried Thanksgiving from another approach.

Working with children for prolonged periods of time will kill adult brain cells and causes adults to say silly sounding things that sound perfectly logical to the person saying them. Mrs. Banks, the hard-working cost-conscious director, ordered a load of dirt instead of expensive sand. The call went something like this:

"This is Rachel Banks, the director of the Spring Hill Avenue Baptist Church day care, and I would like a load of dirt delivered today."

"Yes, Ma'am."

"Now, it has to be clean dirt."

"Ma'am? Clean dirt?"

One of the activities of our day care was the Christmas program—usually a shepherd play with lots of Christmas music. A shepherd play is a three-act play. The first act shows Mary and Joseph as weary travellers arriving in Bethlehem, with Mary about to have the baby Jesus, only to find there's no room at the inn; but the kindly innkeeper says, "Let them use our stable out back."

The next scene is of a bunch of boys dressed in flannel bathrobes and cloth headbands; one little boy stood out from the rest as his headband had a Nike "Swoosh" across it. They were carrying wooden staffs (usually borrowed canes). The teacher had to keep reminding her shepherds not to swordfight with them.

Well, as luck would have it, angels appear unto the shepherds and proclaim that Jesus is born and tell where to find Him. Now, the trick here is to have the angels appear serenely and gracefully as possible, not stumbling, pushing or fighting, and hopefully not swaying absentmindedly, holding up the hem of their white angel garb to reveal to the laughing audience and the mortified teacher the color of their underwear. Somehow the angels are always girls. The only other girl's part is Mary; all the rest of the parts are masculine—Joseph, the innkeeper, the shepherds, and the wise men. The wise men, who just have a walk-on part, are usually the least sedate of the class; they are on stage the least amount of time, so as to minimize the amount of clowning around.

One part so far not mentioned is the star that leads the wise men to Jesus. Now, a lot of churches just use a lighted Christmas tree star that hangs over the table like a neon beacon, revealing that this is the place of the nativity scene. But not our church—we had a boy carefully concealed in the choir loft just behind the stage. As the narrator said, "And a star appeared in the east," that was his cue to stand up and walk to the center of the stage with an enormous yellow paste-board star attached to his head, with a hole cut in the center for his face. At least that's the way it went in rehearsal.

On the day of the performance, the boy decided to give his part more impact. So, on his cue, "And a star appeared in the east," he stood up and quickly climbed to the top of the bar-like railing that separated the choir loft from the stage, and jumped into the middle of the stage. He was greeted with peels of laughter from the audience and a look from his teacher that held a promise of retribution.

After the performance, sealed with the exclamation point of a falling star, the children and parents returned to the classrooms for the reception, where refreshments were provided.

11
THE GOING AWAY PARTY

My time of working at the church was coming to an end. I had received a better job offer, and I felt it was time to move on. When Mrs. Banks heard about me leaving, she decided to give me a going-away party. It was to be a covered dish luncheon.

The ladies had outdone themselves. They even had a cake with "Good Luck Brother Dan" written in blue icing on a white background. The party was set up in the music room. They had pushed two of the preschool tables together, end to end. Twelve of the small chairs were placed in a semicircle in front of the table. Most of these were occupied by teachers and office personnel. The only thing that worried me was how I was going to get up from my undersized chair.

As the guest of honor, I was to be first in line at the food table. I felt as if everyone was watching to see how much I would put on my plate. My reputation as a big eater, which my protruding stomach gave proof to, was no help. If I ate a modest amount to be polite, it would be an insult to their delicious cuisine and the amount of work they had put into it. On the other hand, if I ate a lot, I would be criticized. I decided to try to hit a happy medium, and just take one spoonful of each dish. This theory sounded good, but as I moved along the food line, I came to three different kinds of potato salad. Now, my love for potato salad was as well known as the fierce competition among the ladies with their closely guarded family recipes. As I stood there, trying to make up my mind whether to just take a healthy portion of one or take a little of all three, I felt I was being watched. When I looked up, I saw three ladies—Miss Lucille, Miss Katie, and Miss Mary—all staring at me. I realized that they had to be the three ladies responsible for the potato salad. The room seemed to grow quiet as I paused. I finally took a good sized spoonful from each one. There was almost an audible sigh of relief from the teachers. Happy with my decision, I moved further down the line to encounter two kinds of coleslaw. Once again, I felt I was being watched, so without looking up, I took a helping of both. Soon, my plate began to look like a model of Mt. Olympus. I also noticed that my paper plate was beginning to sag from the sheer weight of the many dishes that I had sampled. As I made my way to my tiny chair, I overheard Mrs. Patty say to the person in line next to her, "Gee, I hope he left some for the rest of us."

I sat on one of the tiny chairs, hoping it wouldn't crumble beneath my weight. It held up. Miss Kim brought me a paper cup of sweet tea, and after I thanked her, she said, "Well, you sure have a healthy appetite." Before I could respond, Mrs. Banks, who was sitting to my left, patted me on the back, saying, "Now, leave Dan alone: This is his special day, and he can eat as much as he wants," making me feel like a small child.

As I was eating and starting to relax, along with feeling full, Miss Lucille approached with her bowl of potato salad, saying, "I know you love potato salad." She plopped a big ladleful on my plate and smiled as she left. About five minutes later, Miss Katie appeared with her bowl, saying, "I just thought you might want to try some that isn't as heavy as Lucille's."

I quickly said, "I don't think I should."

"Why—don't you like my potato salad?" she inquired with a frown.

"No, I love your potato salad. It's just—"

"That's more like it," she said, dropping two big spoonfuls on my plate with a victorious smile.

As I was trying to finish up the last of my salad, Miss Mary blindsided me and started scraping out the remains of her bowl onto my now soggy paper plate. As I looked up at her with a bewildered look, she just shrugged her shoulders and said, "It wasn't enough to take home."

After I had finished my lunch and was sitting there wondering how in the world I was going to get up, Mrs. Elsie, who had agreed to stay in the office and answer the phone during the party, announced I had a call from my wife. All eyes turned toward me, making me feel even more awkward. My first thought as I struggled to rise with a full stomach was, "I hope I don't make a funny noise!" When I finally managed to stand up, I was greeted with applause—as a joke, I'm sure. I left the room with as much dignity as possible.

When I answered the phone, my wife Gayle greeted me, "Dan, I have to work late, so I won't be home for supper. But don't worry: I made you a big bowl of potato salad and left it in the refrigerator. Try not to eat too much."

"Thanks, honey. . . . Potato salad . . . I can't wait. See you later."

As I began to make my way back to the party, I thought about the beautiful cake they had made for me. I had to go back in there and eat a piece. Well, there's one thing I knew for sure—I was going to eat it standing up!

12
BUT SERIOUSLY...

Sometimes, late in October, when the weather was cool and I would be alone working in the auditorium, the sun would come out from behind the clouds and its light would burst in through the stained glass windows and light up the walnut pews at Springhill Avenue with such a luster of autumn color that it would overwhelm me. I would sink right down into the nearest pew and know at that moment that Jesus is Lord, standing at the right hand of God, very much in control. It is at such times that I can feel God's presence and know that He wants us to be happy.